RAMEN

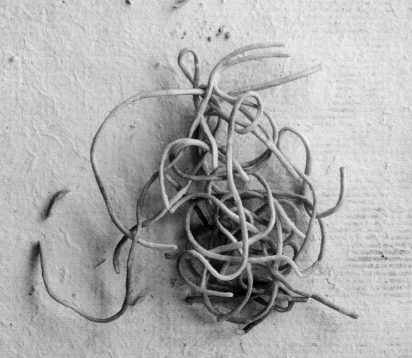

RAMEN

Recipes for ramen and other Asian noodle soups

RYLAND PETERS & SMALL
LONDON • NEW YORK

Senior designer Sonya Nathoo
Commissioning editor Stephanie Milner
Production manager Gordana Simakovic
Art director Leslie Harrington
Editorial director Julia Charles
Publisher Cindy Richards

Indexer Vanessa Bird

First published in 2017 by
Ryland Peters & Small
20–21 Jockey's Fields
London WC1R 4BW
and
341 E 116th St
New York NY 10029
www.rylandpeters.com

10 9 8 7 6 5 4 3 2 1

Recipe collection compiled by Stephanie Milner
Text copyright © Miranda Ballard, Kimiko Barber, Jordan
Bourke, Ross Dobson, Nicola Graimes, Dunja Gulin, Jackie
Kearney, Uyen Luu, Claire and Lucy Macdonald, Louise
Pickford, Belinda Williams and Ryland Peters & Small 2017

Design and photographs copyright © Ryland Peters & Small
2017, see right for full image credits

ISBN: 978-1-84975-815-4

Printed in China

A CIP record for this book is available from the British Library.

US Library of Congress Cataloging-in-Publication Data has
been applied for.

Notes:
• Both British (Metric) and American (Imperial plus
US cups) measurements are included in these recipes for
your convenience, however it is important to work with one
set of measurements and not alternate between the two
within a recipe.
• All spoon measurements are level unless otherwise
specified.
• All eggs are medium (UK) or large (US), unless
specified as large, in which case US extra-large should be
used. Uncooked or partially cooked eggs should not be
served to the very old, frail, young children, pregnant women
or those with compromised immune systems.
• Ovens should be preheated to the specified temperatures.
We recommend using an oven thermometer. If using a
fan-assisted oven, adjust temperatures according to the
manufacturer's instructions.
• When a recipe calls for the grated zest of citrus fruit, buy
unwaxed fruit and wash well before using. If you can only find
treated fruit, scrub well in warm soapy water before using.
• To sterilize preserving jars, wash them in hot, soapy
water and rinse in boiling water. Place in a large saucepan
and cover with hot water. With the saucepan lid on, bring the
water to a boil and continue boiling for 15 minutes. Turn off
the heat and leave the jars in the hot water until just before
they are to be filled. Invert the jars onto a clean dish towel
to dry. Sterilize the lids for 5 minutes, by boiling or according
to the manufacturer's instructions. Jars should be filled and
sealed while they are still hot.

Food photography by:
Tara Fisher; Pages 33
Mowie Kay; Pages 14, 17, 21, 30, 36, 37, 53, 62
William Reavell; Pages 29
Ian Wallace; Pages 1, 2, 5, 7–12, 15, 18, 19, 31, 34, 38,
42–50, 54–57, 61, 64
Clare Winfield; Pages 3, 22–26, 41, 58

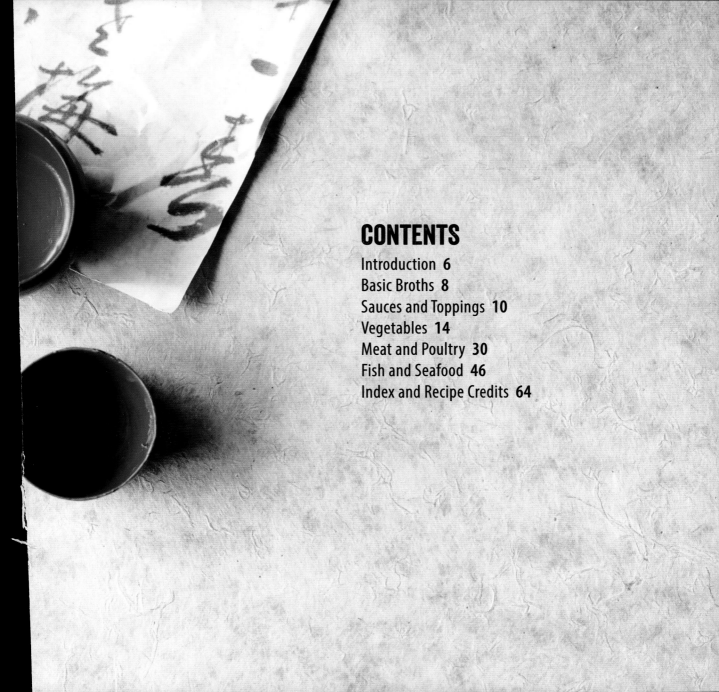

CONTENTS

Introduction 6
Basic Broths 8
Sauces and Toppings 10
Vegetables 14
Meat and Poultry 30
Fish and Seafood 46
Index and Recipe Credits 64

INTRODUCTION

'Ramen' is the Japanese term for any noodle soup dish prepared with a fish, meat or miso broth. Noodles are drenched in deep, clear broths that are rich in nutrients, flavour and often pack a punch of chilli heat. They are then adorned with a variety of toppings that vary from soft- and hard-boiled/cooked eggs to dried, fried onions and shallots, and spicy Sambal dressings to thinly sliced fresh vegetables. Layers of braised or crispy meat and puffed tofu can also be added to create a truly delicious bowlful to feed the soul.

Typically there are four types of base broth for ramen: 'shio' (salt), 'shoyu' (soy), 'tonkotsu' (pork) and miso, as well as a host of other styles from around Asia. Broth can be made fairly quickly from pastes and base dried ingredients but others require a longer time to stew, to draw flavour from ingredients and develop richness of texture and smoothness of mouthfeel.

Shio ramen contain a light-coloured broth made from dried seafood, seaweed and other salty ingredients. The Dashi Broth on page 8 is ideal to pour over noodles to create an umami-rich shio ramen in dishes such as Mushroom Udon on page 19, Kombu Broth with Tempura on page 28 and Shio Ramen with Pork and Eggs on page 43.

Shoyu ramen are the most common of all ramen, and in fact, almost all ramen have a shoyu base in that they usually contain soy. But it is the high quantity of soy used that makes a ramen shoyu. Mung Bean Vegetable Noodle Soup on page 27 and Ramen with Tempura Shrimp on page 51 are typical of shoyu ramen.

Tonkotsu ramen is made from a base of bones, often roasted, then boiled with other ingredients to release their collagen properties. Bone broths take longer to prepare than shio or miso broths but are well worth the wait. Try Traditional Vietnamese Pho on page 32 or Chicken Noodle Soup on page 44 – you won't be disappointed.

Finally, miso ramen are made using fermented soy bean pastes that ferment over time in large pots. Miso comes in various forms, most commonly in brown, white or red paste but it is worth seeking out more unusual varieties that can be found in Asian supermarkets and online. Miso broths can transform most ramen in this book into vegetarian dishes, substituting broths that use meat or fish bases for miso. Classic dishes include Sapporo Miso Ramen with Chicken on page 31 and Salmon and Miso Soup on page 63.

Each type of broth is described in the pages that follow, as well as a glossary of ingredients and basic recipes for toppings, sauces and dressings. Try making your own Deep-fried Shallots on page 12 and Deep-fried Puffed Tofu on page 13; or sauces such as Sambal Olek on page 10 and Jeow Marg Leng on page 10. The beauty of these noodle soups is that there are no rules – the combination of ingredients is down to your personal preference and can be altered however you see fit. Be encouraged to try new things with these ideas for Vietnamese pho, Japanese udon, Malay laksa, Burmese mohinga, Cambodian num bánh chok and Thai tom yum. There are endless possibilities for creating these hot, spicy, sweet or smooth noodle broths.

BASIC BROTHS

Many of the recipes in this book can be made following the ingredients given on the page but you could build your own perfect ramen using one of these basic broths, filling your bowl with your favourite noodle and selecting from the variety of toppings and sauces that follow.

DASHI BROTH

15 g/1 tablespoon chopped dried kombu (seaweed)

15 g/1 tablespoon dried bonito flakes

MAKES 1 LITRE/2 PINTS

Pour 1.25 litres/2¹/₂ pints cold water into a saucepan, add the dried kombu and set aside for 30 minutes to soften. Bring the mixture to the boil over a medium heat, removing any scum that appears on the surface, then reduce the heat and simmer gently for 10 minutes.

Remove the pan from the heat, stir in the bonito flakes and allow the broth to cool.

Strain and use immediately or chill until required. The broth will keep stored in an airtight container for 3 days in the fridge or can be frozen for up to 1 month.

VARIATION: For a vegetarian version, omit the bonito flakes and increase the kombu to a total of 20 g/ 1 heaped tablespoon.

NOTE: Dashi is a Japanese stock and forms the underbelly of many Japanese dishes. It has a very distinctive, smokey flavour and sea-water aroma.

VEGETABLE BROTH

2 onions, halved
2 leeks, thickly sliced
1 fennel bulb, halved
4 celery sticks/ribs, thickly sliced
4 carrots, peeled and thickly sliced
1–2 bay leaves
a few sprigs of fresh thyme
a small bunch of fresh parsley
10 white peppercorns
sea salt

MAKES 1.5 LITRES/3 PINTS

Put all the ingredients in a large saucepan and top up with 2.5 litres/5 pints water. Cover the pan with a lid, bring to the boil over a medium heat, then reduce to a simmer. Let it simmer for 1¹/₂ hours, removing the lid for the last 30 minutes of cooking time so it can reduce a little.

Remove the pan from the heat and strain into a container to cool. Use straight away or portion into bags or containers to refrigerate or freeze.

NOTE: If you prefer a slightly richer flavour, brown the vegetables in a tablespoon of butter before adding the liquid to the pan.

BONE BROTH

15 g/1 tablespoon butter

3 celery sticks/ribs, including stalks, roughly chopped

3 whole carrots, untrimmed and roughly chopped

2 white onions, roughly chopped

2 garlic cloves, roughly chopped

4–5 beef or pork rib bones, chopped into single bone pieces

a big pinch each of cracked black pepper and sea salt

2 bay leaves

a sprig of fresh thyme

2 tablespoons apple cider vinegar

MAKES 500–750 ML/ 1–1½ PINTS

Heat the butter in a large saucepan set over a high heat. Throw in the celery, carrots, onions and garlic, and stir in the melted butter for 1–2 minutes, until it begins to brown.

Add the bones and all of the seasoning, then the apple cider vinegar and enough water to come 2.5 cm/1 inch above the bones. Keep the heat to high to bring to the boil for 10 minutes, then reduce the heat to the lowest setting, half cover with the lid and simmer for at least 4 hours, or 8–10 hours if you can. Check the pan every hour and top up the water if it drops below half the height of the solid ingredients and bones. Stir the mixture as well to make sure it isn't catching on the bottom.

Remove from the heat and strain into a container to cool. Use it straight away or portion it into bags or containers to refrigerate or freeze. It will thicken to a jelly when chilled.

CHICKEN BROTH

2 kg/4 lbs. chicken pieces, preferably free range

a bunch of spring onions/ scallions, trimmed and chopped

1 whole head garlic, cloves roughly chopped

a 5-cm/2-inch piece of fresh ginger, peeled, sliced and pounded

1 red onion, roughly chopped

salt, to taste

MAKES 2 LITRES/4 PINTS

Put the chicken pieces in a large saucepan with the spring onions/scallions, garlic, ginger and red onion and pour over 3 litres/5½ pints cold water. Set the pan over a medium heat and bring the mixture slowly to the boil, skimming the surface to remove any scum.

Reduce the heat and simmer gently for 1½ hours until the stock is full of flavour.

Strain and discard the chicken pieces and vegetables. Return the stock to the pan and simmer until reduced to 2 litres/4 pints. Add a little salt to taste.

Use immediately or cool and chill overnight. The stock will keep, stored in an airtight container, for 3 days in the fridge or can be frozen for up to 1 month. Skim off any residual fat from the top before using each time.

SAUCES AND TOPPINGS

Ramen just isn't ramen without a variety of toppings available to sprinkle over piping hot bowls of glistening broth. While many can be store-bought it feels indulgent to make your own toppings at home.

SAMBAL OLEK

5 Asian shallots, chopped
25 g/scant ¹/₄ cup chopped large red chillies/chiles (deseeded, if desired)
2 large garlic cloves, sliced
1 lemongrass stalk, trimmed and chopped
1 teaspoon ground turmeric

2 tablespoons peanut oil
1 tablespoon tamarind paste
1 tablespoon light soy sauce
1 tablespoon caster/granulated sugar

MAKES 125 ML/½ CUP

Put the shallots, chillies/chiles, garlic, lemongrass and turmeric in a food processor and blend until smooth, adding 2 teaspoons of the oil if necessary.

Heat the remaining oil in a wok or large frying pan/skillet set over a very low heat and gently fry the paste for about 10 minutes, until really fragrant. Stir in the tamarind paste, soy sauce and sugar and cook, stirring continuously, for 5 minutes until the oil comes to the top.

Remove the pan from the heat and leave to cool completely. Use as required or store in a sterilized glass bottle or jar in the fridge for up to 1 month.

NOTE: This has a lovely depth of flavour to it with a hint of tamarind, which is very fragrant – perfect with soups.

JEOW MARG LENG

6 large cherry tomatoes
6 garlic cloves, unpeeled
1 large shallot, unpeeled
1–2 small red bird's eye chillies/chiles
¹/₂ teaspoon caster/granulated sugar

1 spring onion/scallion, trimmed and finely chopped
1 tablespoon chopped fresh coriander/cilantro
2 teaspoons lime juice
1 teaspoon fish sauce

SERVES 4

Heat a stovetop ridged grill pan over a medium heat until smoking and then grill the tomatoes for 15–20 minutes until completely charred and softened. Set aside to cool, then peel and discard the blackened skin.

Repeat with the garlic cloves, whole shallot and chillies/chiles, cooking them until the skins are charred and the flesh softened. Allow them to cool, then peel and discard the skin. Chop the vegetables and put in a mortar. Pound to a rough paste with a pestle.

Transfer the paste to a mixing bowl and stir in the sugar, spring onion/scallion, coriander/cilantro, lime juice and fish sauce. Store in a sterilized glass jar in the fridge for up to 3 weeks and use as required.

NOTE: This is a cooked tomato salsa that is wonderfully spicy and smoky. It works well stirred into soups.

CHILLI/CHILI OIL

30 g/6 whole dried chillies/
chiles
250 ml/1 cup peanut oil

*a sterilized glass bottle with
an airtight cap*

MAKES 250 ML/1 CUP

Put the chillies/chiles in a bowl, cover with hot water and soak for 30 minutes until slightly softened. Drain well.

Put the chillies/chiles in a food processor and blend to a rough paste. Transfer to a small saucepan, pour in the oil and bring gently to the boil over a medium heat. Boil for 1 minute. Remove from the heat and let cool completely.

Strain the oil into a sterilized glass bottle and seal. Keep in the fridge for up to 1 month and use as required.

VEGAN FISH SAUCE

50 g/2 oz. seaweed (such as
laver, dulse or arame),
cut into small strips
500 ml/2 cups light soy
sauce or tamari
8 black peppercorns

2 garlic cloves, peeled
1 dried Chinese or shiitake
mushroom

*a sterilized glass bottle with
an airtight cap*

MAKES 750 ML/3 CUPS

Put the dried seaweed in a pan and pour over 500 ml/ 1 pint of water. Bring to the boil, then simmer until the water has reduced by half. Set aside for 1 hour.

Strain the liquid into a bowl. Rinse the pan and add the soy sauce, peppercorns, garlic and dried mushroom. Bring to a simmer and add the seaweed reduction. Simmer for 30–40 minutes until the mixture has reduced by half.

Strain and store in the fridge and use as required.

QUICK KIMCHI

350 g/6 cups Chinese
cabbage, thinly sliced
4 teaspoons sea salt
2 tablespoons caster/
granulated sugar
1 tablespoon dried Korean
chilli/hot red pepper
flakes
2 teaspoons freshly grated
ginger
2 garlic cloves, crushed

2 tablespoons fish sauce
2 teaspoons sesame seeds,
toasted
2 spring onions/scallions,
trimmed and thinly sliced

*a 500-ml/1-pint capacity
sterilized glass jar with an
airtight lid*

MAKES 1 JAR

Put the cabbage in a bowl and stir in the salt. Add enough water to cover and leave to soak for 30 minutes. Drain well and squeeze out excess water using a clean kitchen cloth.

Mix together the sugar, chilli/hot red pepper flakes, ginger, garlic, fish sauce and sesame seeds in a small bowl to make a thin paste. Stir the paste into the cabbage with the spring onions/scallions, cover and leave to marinate for 1 hour. Serve, or store for up to 2 days in the fridge.

CRUSHED ROASTED NUTS

100 g/1 cup raw peanuts or cashews
MAKES ABOUT 100 G/1 CUP

Preheat the oven to 170°C (325°F) Gas 3.

Spread the nuts onto a baking sheet and roast in the preheated oven for 10 minutes. Remove from the oven and immediately wrap the nuts in a clean kitchen cloth. Set aside and allow the steam to build for a minute before rubbing them within the cloth to remove any loose skins. Cool completely then roughly crush in a pestle and mortar to a chunky texture. Use immediately or store in an airtight container for up to 1 week.

DEEP-FRIED SHALLOTS

12 Asian shallots, thinly sliced
vegetable oil, for deep frying
MAKES ABOUT 50 G/⅓ CUP

Pour the oil into a wok or saucepan about 5 cm/2 inches up the side of the pan and set over a medium heat. Test the temperature of the pan by dropping a cube of bread into the hot oil – it should crisp within 30 seconds.

Deep-fry the shallots, in batches, for 2–3 minutes, until crisp and golden, but do not allow the shallots to burn or they will become bitter. Remove with a slotted spoon and drain on paper towels.

Serve immediately or store in an airtight container for up to 2 weeks. If they become a little soggy, crisp them up in a dry frying pan/skillet as necessary.

TWO WAYS WITH TOFU

1 block medium or firm tofu,
    drained and cubed
flavourless oil, for deep-
    frying or coating

DEEP-FRIED PUFFED TOFU
cornflour/cornstarch, for
    dusting

MARINATED TOFU
1 tablespoon flavourless oil
1 teaspoon thinly sliced
    fresh ginger, Chinese
    five-spice or chopped red
    chilli/chile

a baking sheet, well-greased

MAKES ABOUT 20

First, pat the tofu cubes dry with paper towels.

Deep-fried Puffed Tofu: Pour the oil into a large pan or
wok and set over a medium–high heat. The oil must be hot
so as not to make the tofu greasy.

Lightly coat the tofu cubes in cornflour/cornstarch before
deep-frying in the hot oil until golden brown.

Once cooled, these puffs can be refrigerated for up to
a week (or frozen).

Marinated Tofu: Pour 1 tablespoon of oil into a small bowl
and add your chosen marinating ingredient. Add the tofu
and gently coat. Set aside for 30 minutes.

Preheat the oven to 180°C (350°F) Gas 4.

Spread the marinated tofu onto the prepared baking
sheet and bake in the preheated oven for 5–10 minutes,
turning pieces occasionally to ensure even cooking. Once
cooled, it can be stored in the fridge for a week (or frozen).

FISHCAKES WITH DILL

300 g/10^1/$_2$ oz. skinless
    white fish fillets, chopped
1 Asian shallot, chopped
1 Bird's Eye chilli/chile
1^1/$_2$ teaspoons white sugar
1 teaspoon baking powder
a pinch of black pepper
2 tablespoons cooking oil,

    plus extra for frying
2 tablespoons fish sauce
1 tablespoon tapioca starch
a handful of fresh dill

a steamer (optional)

SERVES 4

Put all the ingredients in a food processor and process
until fine and well combined. Transfer the mixture to a
bowl, cover and allow to rest for 1–2 hours or overnight –
in which case, put it in the refrigerator.

Rub a little oil onto your hands. Pull small pieces off the
rested mixture and roll into balls between your hands.
Alternatively, shape the mixture into 1 large or 2 small
patties.

Steam the balls or patties for 5 minutes in a steamer. They
can then be refrigerated or frozen, to be fried at a later
date. You can also poach them in broth for noodle soups.

To serve, heat a dash of oil in a frying pan/skillet and fry
the balls or fishcakes, stirring or turning a couple of times,
until golden brown all over. Leave the balls whole, but
slice the patties.

VEGETABLES

UDON NOODLE SOUP WITH CRISPY TOFU

1/2 block firm tofu (about
    200 g/6¹/₂ oz.), drained
5 tablespoons tamari or dark
    soy sauce
3 tablespoons mirin
2 tablespoons coconut palm
    sugar
200 g/6¹/₂ oz. mangetout/
    snow peas
400 g/14 oz. udon noodles
    or rice noodles
1.5 litres/3 pints Dashi Broth
    (page 8) or fish or
    vegetable stock
a 5-cm/2-inch piece of fresh
    ginger, peeled and cut into
    chunks
1 tablespoon sunflower oil
2 spring onions/scallions,
    sliced
sesame seeds, to serve

SERVES 4

This is one of those simple, comforting and totally delicious Japanese noodle soups that you will find yourself making all the time. If you are pushed for time, you could simply marinate the tofu briefly before frying. Good-quality Japanese udon noodles are available in most supermarkets; they are made with wheat flour, so if you are avoiding wheat, use rice noodles instead.

Wrap the drained tofu in a clean kitchen cloth and very gently squeeze to remove excess water. Remove the cloth and slice into 16 pieces of equal size.

In a wide bowl, combine together the tamari or dark soy sauce, mirin and coconut palm sugar. Add in the tofu, cover with the marinade and leave to infuse for 25 minutes.

Bring a pot of salted water to the boil, add in the mangetout/snow peas and cook for 2 minutes, then remove (reserving the water for the udon) and plunge into cold water. Cook the udon noodles according to the packet instructions, then rinse under running cold water.

Remove the tofu from the marinade (reserve the marinade) and shake off any excess. Add the dashi and ginger to a small saucepan, almost bring to the boil and add in the reserved tofu marinade, then reduce the heat to a gentle simmer.

Place a frying pan/skillet over a medium-high heat, and add in 1 tablespoon of sunflower oil. When hot, add in the tofu and fry for 1 minute on each side until golden. Remove, drain and keep warm.

When ready to serve, add the udon and mangetout/snow peas to the stock until warmed through, then immediately ladle into bowls (avoiding the ginger), top with the tofu, spring onions/scallions and sesame seeds and serve.

MISO RAMEN WITH STIR-FRIED VEGETABLES

3 tablespoons red miso paste

1 tablespoon light soy sauce

$1/2$ teaspoon white sugar

1.25 litres/$2^1/2$ pints vegetable stock

200 g/7 oz. ramen or thin egg noodles

1 tablespoon light olive oil

2 teaspoons sesame oil

2 teaspoons finely sliced fresh ginger

2 shallots, thinly sliced

2 leeks, julienned

$1/4$ Savoy cabbage, finely shredded

$1/4$ red cabbage, finely shredded

SERVES 4

Ramen are hearty and comforting. They are often full of fresh and earthy cold-weather vegetables, sometimes with the addition of freshly shucked sweetcorn. The broths themselves are generally made with a base of simple stock and soy sauce or miso. This prepared, soya bean paste is probably the most essential Japanese food item with a very strong 'umami' (savoury) component. Easily found in the Asian foods aisle at your supermarket or a speciality food store, it will keep for a long time in the fridge. The noodles, although common in Japan, are Chinese wheat-based noodles and, when bought dried, are a very handy staple.

Combine the miso paste, soy sauce, sugar and stock in a large saucepan set over a medium heat and warm until the miso has completely dissolved. Keep warm over a low heat. Cook the noodles according to the packet instructions. Drain well and divide between 4 warmed serving bowls.

Put the oils in a wok or large frying pan/skillet set over a high heat. Add the ginger and shallots and cook for just a few seconds to flavour the oil. Add the leeks and cabbage and stir-fry for 2 minutes, until the vegetables are crisp and glistening with oil.

Ladle the warm miso mixture over the noodles and top with the stir-fried vegetables. Serve immediately.

MUSHROOM UDON

200 g/7 oz. dried udon
noodles

1.5 litres/3 pints Dashi Broth
(page 8)

50 ml/scant ¼ cup dark soy
sauce

3 tablespoons mirin

2 tablespoons sake

500 g/1 lb. mixed mushrooms,
including shiitake, oyster
and enoki

150 g/1 cup sugar snap peas,
trimmed and cut in half
lengthways

200 g/2 cups cubed silken/
soft tofu

2 tablespoons dried wakame
seaweed

seven-spice powder,
to serve

SERVES 4

This is a light, delicately flavoured mushroom soup. Vegetarians may want to make a version of dashi without the bonito flakes — see page 8 for alternatives. You should be able to buy most of the mushrooms fairly readily from larger supermarkets or online, but could substitute like for like with any mushrooms that you are able to find.

Plunge the noodles into a saucepan of boiling water and cook for 4–5 minutes or until al dente. Drain, refresh under cold water and shake dry. Set aside.

Pour the broth, soy sauce, mirin and sake into a saucepan set over a medium heat and bring to the boil. Add the mushrooms except the enoki and simmer gently for 5 minutes until the mushrooms are tender. Stir in the sugar snap peas and enoki mushrooms and simmer for 2 minutes.

Divide the noodles between warmed bowls and top with the tofu and seaweed. Pour the soup over the top, sprinkle with seven-spice powder and serve at once.

CHILLED SOMEN NOODLES WITH WASABI AND DIPPING SAUCE

about 400 g/1 lb. dried
   somen noodles

SOY DIPPING SAUCE

8 dried shiitake mushrooms
250 ml/1 cup Dashi Broth
   (page 8)
125 ml/¹⁄₂ cup mirin or dry
   sherry
60 ml/¹⁄₄ cup soy sauce

TO SERVE

a 3-cm/1-inch piece of fresh
   ginger, finely grated
1 sheet dried nori seaweed,
   thinly sliced
8 spring onions/scallions,
   thinly sliced diagonally
1 baby cucumber, peeled and
   thinly sliced

SERVES 4–6

Cold ramen is the perfect late-night snack that's also a refreshing meal. This dish brings with it a summer soothingness for warm evenings when only a chilled noodle soup will do. Serve the white noodles floating in a big bowl of iced water and toppings and dipping sauce on the side.

Put the shiitake mushrooms into a bowl and cover with hot water. Leave to rehydrate for at least 15 minutes or until softened. Drain, reserving the soaking liquid. Cut off and discard the hard stems and thinly slice the caps.

Put the dashi into a saucepan and heat gently until almost boiling. Reduce the heat immediately, add the mirin and soy sauce and return to the boil. Turn off the heat and let cool to room temperature. You may prepare up to this point the day before and refrigerate until ready to use.

Bring a large saucepan of water to the boil and add the noodles, one bundle at a time. Stir with chopsticks each time you add a bundle to make sure they separate. Watch the saucepan carefully and stand by with a glass of cold water ready.

When the water begins to boil over, add the cold water. This is called 'bikkuri mizu' (meaning 'surprise water') and it is used to make the outside and inside of the noodles cook at the same speed. Return to the boil and turn off the heat. Drain and rinse the noodles under cold running water, drain again and chill.

To serve, float the noodles in a large glass bowl or separate small bowls, filled with ice and water. Put the ginger, seaweed, spring onions/scallions and cucumber on a separate plate and put the soy dipping sauce in a bowl. Guests can choose their own combinations of ingredients at the table.

300 g/11 oz. dried flat rice
   noodles
400 g/14 oz. firm tofu, rinsed,
   drained and cut into
   bite-sized pieces
6 garlic cloves, thinly sliced
a 7.5-cm/3-inch piece of fresh
   ginger, finely diced
2 small carrots, sliced
   diagonally
1 small courgette/ zucchini,
   sliced diagonally
$^1/_2$ small cauliflower, cut into
   small florets
120 g/4 oz. green/French
   beans, chopped
1 litre/2 pints vegetable stock
2–3 lemongrass stalks,
   bruised
6 kaffir lime leaves
800 ml/3$^1/_2$ cups coconut
   milk
6 tablespoons light soy sauce
   or tamari
4 tablespoons Vegan Fish
   Sauce (page 11)
salt, to taste
2 large red chillies/chiles,
   sliced
150 g/2$^3/_4$ cups beansprouts
a small handful of fresh
   coriander/cilantro leaves
1 lime, halved

a baking sheet, greased

SERVES 4–6

FRAGRANT VEGETABLE SIAM SOUP

Noodle soup is everywhere in south-east Asia, and especially in Thailand and Laos. The little roadside stalls set up a few plastic chairs and tables alongside their wok and cart, and, hey presto, you have an al fresco noodle-soup café. Unlike many other street foods, this one requires the diner to take a seat in order to eat. An ice-cold beer complements the level of spice in this bowl.

Preheat the oven to 190°C (375°F) Gas 5.

Put the noodles in a large bowl. Add hand-hot water to cover. Soak for 5–10 minutes until soft but with plenty of bite. Rinse, drain and set aside.

Put the tofu on the prepared baking sheet. Bake for 10–15 minutes or until starting to crisp and turn golden brown. (Alternatively, you can fry the tofu in 2–3 tablespoons oil, then drain on paper towels.)

Heat the oil in a large pan over a medium heat and add the garlic and ginger. Cook for 3–4 minutes or until they start to turn golden. Add the vegetables to the pan and cook for 2–3 minutes, then add the vegetable stock and 1 litre/2 pints of boiling water.

Add the lemongrass to taste and lime leaves, then add the coconut milk, soy sauce and vegan fish sauce. Add salt to taste.

Bring to the boil, then add the tofu. If you want to make the soup a little spicy, add the chillies/chiles. The broth evaporates easily and you want plenty to cover the noodles and vegetables, so add more water if needed. Bring to the boil, then set aside. Remove the lemongrass.

Put a large handful of noodles in each serving bowl, then ladle over the soup, ensuring there is a mixture of vegetables and tofu in each bowl, and the liquid covers almost all the noodles. Sprinkle over the beansprouts, coriander/cilantro and sliced chillies/chiles, then add a squeeze of lime juice.

6 red chillies/chiles, stems removed

2 small red onions (unpeeled), halved

2 lemongrass stalks

1 tablespoon paprika

vegetable oil (if needed)

1 litre/2 pints vegetable stock

3 tablespoons Vegan Fish Sauce (page 11) or light soy sauce with a pinch of seaweed flakes

2 tablespoons tamarind pulp or 2 teaspoons tamarind concentrate/paste

1–2 teaspoons salt, to taste

1–2 tablespoons soft brown sugar or rice syrup, to taste

375 g/13 oz. thick round rice noodles

FRESH TOPPINGS

1/2 cucumber, halved lengthways

1 fresh lotus root, peeled

1/2 pineapple

a handful of Vietnamese mint leaves

a handful of laksa leaves

1 small red onion, thinly sliced

1 bird's eye chilli/chile, finely chopped

SERVES 4–6

ASSAM LAKSA

There are lots of great vegetarian cafés in Penang, Malaysia, and many offer their own version of a vegetarian Assam laksa, a much-famed dish on the island. This recipe relies on vegan fish sauce or a pinch of dried seaweed to add flavour to the popular hot-and-sour noodle broth, usually made with mackerel. Lotus root, with its crunchy texture adds exotic flair but can be substituted with water chestnuts.

Preheat the oven to 210°C (410°F) Gas 6.

Put the chillies/chiles and onions on a baking sheet and roast for 10–15 minutes until starting to blacken at the edges. Let cool, then peel the onions.

Put the lemongrass in a food processor and add the paprika, roasted chillies/chiles and onions, then blend to a paste, adding a little oil if needed to thin the mixture. Put the spice paste in a wok or large pan over a high heat and cook for 2 minutes.

Add the stock, 1 litre/2 pints of water, the vegan fish sauce and tamarind to the pan. Bring to the boil over a high heat and simmer briskly for 8–10 minutes. Add salt and sugar to taste.

Meanwhile, soak the noodles in hot water for 10 minutes, then drain in a colander.

To prepare the fresh toppings, using a teaspoon, scrape out the watery seeds from the centre of the cucumber. Thinly slice the cucumber and lotus root. Blanch the sliced lotus root in boiling water for 1 minute, then set aside. Using a sharp knife, cut the top and bottom off the pineapple, then stand it on one end and cut off the peel and the 'eyes'. Cut the pineapple in half lengthways and cut out the core. Chop the flesh.

Divide the noodles among serving bowls, then add a selection of the fresh toppings. Ladle over the broth to ensure the noodles are well covered. Serve.

375 g/13 oz. mung bean
  noodles or rice
  vermicelli noodles
1 tablespoon toasted sesame
  oil
1 tablespoon vegetable oil
8 garlic cloves, crushed
1 tablespoon finely chopped
  fresh galangal or ginger
2 litres/4 pints vegetable
  stock or water
2 tablespoons Vegan Fish
  Sauce (page 11), soy sauce
  or tamari
3 tablespoons light soy sauce
  or tamari
1 teaspoon soft brown sugar
1 lemongrass stalk, bruised
  with a rolling pin
1/8 white cabbage, shredded
1/8 dark green cabbage or
  100 g/3 cups kale,
  shredded
1 carrot, coarsely grated or
  julienned
120 g/2 cups beansprouts
4 spring onions/scallions,
  sliced (including the green
  parts)
freshly squeezed juice of
  1 lime
2 red chillies/chiles, thinly
  sliced to garnish

SERVES 4

MUNG BEAN VEGETABLE NOODLE SOUP

It's hard to turn a corner in Thailand without seeing a noodle soup vendor, and it soon becomes a staple dish in any traveller's diet. The traditional vegetable noodle soup uses mung bean or thread noodles (sometimes called 'glass' or 'cellophane' noodles), but you could substitute any rice noodles. You can make the soup more substantial by adding Deep-fried puffed tofu (page 13) as a topping at the end, but the simplicity of this dish makes for a quick and filling lunch.

Put the noodles in a large bowl and cover with boiling water. Leave for 4–5 minutes until the noodles are soft. Rinse, drain and set aside.

Heat the sesame and vegetable oils in a large pan over a medium heat and cook the garlic and galangal for 3–4 minutes, until golden brown and starting to crisp. (At this stage, you could put the crispy fried garlic and galangal back into a mortar, bash them a little to make a rough paste, then return to the pan.) Add the vegetable stock and bring to the boil. Add the vegan fish sauce, soy sauce, sugar and bruised lemongrass. Bring to the boil, then simmer for 5 minutes.

Add the shredded cabbages, carrot, beansprouts, three-quarters of the chopped spring onions/scallions and the noodles, then return to the boil and immediately remove from the heat. Remove the lemongrass and add the lime juice.

To serve, pour into large, deep bowls and top each bowl with the remaining spring onions/scallions and sliced chillies/chiles.

100 g/3^{1}/$_{2}$ oz. dried soba or
    udon noodles
4 dried shiitake mushrooms
a 12-cm/4^{3}/$_{4}$-inch strip of
    kombu seaweed
2 small leeks
2 small carrots
2-cm/^{3}/$_{4}$-inch piece of fresh
    ginger, crushed
3 garlic cloves
4 tablespoons dark sesame
    oil
tamari, to taste
2 tablespoons toasted
    sesame seeds

TEMPURA
110 ml/^{1}/$_{2}$ cup ice-cold water
70 g /^{1}/$_{2}$ cup chilled
    unbleached plain/
    all-purpose flour, plus extra
    for coating
^{1}/$_{4}$ teaspoon ground turmeric
220 ml/1 scant cup sunflower
    oil, for frying
a selection of vegetables
    (broccoli, courgette/
    zucchini, pumpkin,
    celeriac/celery root, sweet
    potato, onion), peeled and
    thinly sliced
sea salt, to season

SERVES 2–4

KOMBU BROTH WITH TEMPURA

A Japanese-style breakfast or lunch that will leave you feeling warm, relaxed and satisfied, and ready to continue with whatever you're doing. Serve in big bowls, sip the soup and use chopsticks to eat the noodles and veggies!

Place the shiitake and kombu in a saucepan and add 1.3 litres/2^{1}/$_{2}$ pints of water. Cover and let boil, then lower to a medium heat and let cook for 10 minutes. Remove the kombu and shiitake (slice the tops and discard stems), and keep the broth.

In a large saucepan, sauté the vegetables, ginger and garlic in the dark sesame oil for a couple of minutes. Add the sliced shiitake and the broth and let boil for 5–10 minutes. Season with plenty of tamari.

Cook the noodles separately until al dente, just before serving. If you cook them in the broth, they will soak up a lot of water and you'll end up with less soup than planned!

To make the batter, in a bowl, quickly mix the ice-cold water and flour with a whisk and add salt to taste and the turmeric. Do not over-mix – some lumps are alright. To make the tempura crispy, it's very important to use cold ingredients, not mix too much and use the batter for frying immediately.

Pat each vegetable slice dry with paper towels and roll into flour before dipping into the tempura so that the batter doesn't slide off. Heat the sunflower oil in a frying pan/skillet and when hot, dip a couple of vegetable pieces in the batter and fry until slightly golden. You will need about 4 pieces of veggies per person. If you feel the batter is too thin and doesn't stick properly to the floured vegetables, add a little more flour.

Drain the tempura vegetables on paper towels and serve immediately. Serve the cooked, drained noodles in the kombu broth sprinkled with the sesame seeds, with the tempura veggies on the side.

SAPPORO MISO RAMEN WITH CHICKEN

2 tablespoons peanut oil

200 g/8 oz. skinless, boneless chicken thighs, thinly sliced

1 onion, thinly sliced lengthways

1 leek, split lengthways, rinsed and finely chopped

1 carrot, julienned

250 g/8 oz. canned sliced bamboo shoots, rinsed and julienned

16 mangetout/snow peas, coarsely chopped

250 g/8 oz. beansprouts, rinsed and trimmed

1 teaspoon soy sauce

4 dried ramen noodle nests

1 litre/2 pints chicken stock

1 garlic clove, finely chopped

1½ tablespoons mirin or dry sherry

4 tablespoons light or medium miso paste

sea salt and freshly ground black pepper, to season

TO SERVE

2 spring onions/scallions, finely chopped

1 tablespoon Chilli/Chili Oil (page 11)

1 tablespoon toasted sesame seeds

SERVES 4

This is a substantial, heart-warming miso soup with a difference from Sapporo, the regional capital of Hokkaido, Japan's northern island. Hokkaido was the equivalent of the 'Wild West frontier' in the mid-19th century, when the new government encouraged large numbers of pioneer farmers and miners to go north in search of a new life. In the harsh and barren winters, non-traditional ingredients such as garlic and chilli oil warmed the bodies and hearts of the new settlers.

Heat the peanut oil in a wok and swirl to coat. Add the chicken, onion, leek, carrot, bamboo shoots, mangetout/snow peas and beansprouts and stir-fry over a high heat for 5 minutes. Season with the soy sauce, then taste and adjust the seasoning with salt and pepper.

Bring a large saucepan of water to the boil, add the noodles and cook for 2 minutes. Drain and transfer to 4 deep soup bowls.

Meanwhile, put the stock into a saucepan and bring to the boil. Add the garlic, mirin and miso paste. Stir thoroughly to dissolve the paste. Ladle the soup over the noodles and top with the stir-fried mixture.

Sprinkle with the spring onions/scallions, chilli/chile oil and sesame seeds, and serve immediately.

2 onions, quartered
  (unpeeled)
2 x 10-cm/4-inch pieces
  of fresh ginger, halved
3 garlic cloves (unpeeled)
2 teaspoons whole black
  peppercorns
2 cinnamon sticks
7 star anise
6 whole cloves
1 black cardamom pod
  (optional)
$1^1/_2$ tablespoons coriander
  seeds
1 kg/$2^1/_4$ lbs. beef bones,
  half with marrow
$2^1/_2$ tablespoons fish sauce
2 tablespoons coconut palm
  sugar
1 tablespoon freshly squeezed
  lime juice
375 g/13 oz. flat rice noodles
150 g/5 oz. beef fillet, very
  thinly sliced
100 g/1 cup beansprouts
3 spring onions/scallions,
  sliced diagonally
1 small handful each of fresh
  coriander/cilantro and mint
  (Thai basil, optional)
2 limes, cut into wedges
2 fresh red chillies/chiles,
  sliced

SERVES 4

TRADITIONAL VIETNAMESE PHO

Vietnamese pho (pronounced 'fuh') is one of these incredibly satisfying south-east Asian dishes that somehow manages to be rich and full of flavour, whilst at the same time being beautifully light and fragrant.

Put a dry frying pan/skillet over a high heat, and when extremely hot add the onions, ginger and garlic. Stir-fry for a few minutes until a little charred. Remove and leave to cool, then peel the ingredients and remove any burnt areas. Put the spices in the same dry pan and set over a medium heat for a few minutes until aromatic.

Put the beef bones in a large pot of cold water and bring to the boil for 5 minutes, discard the water, rinse the bones and the pot, then return them to the pot together with the onion, ginger, garlic, spices and 3 litres/$5^1/_2$ pints water – enough to generously cover the bones. Bring to the boil, reduce the heat and simmer with the lid off for $2^1/_2$–3 hours until the liquid has reduced by a third. Strain the broth through a muslin- or cheesecloth-lined sieve/strainer and return the liquid to the pot. Add in the fish sauce, coconut palm sugar and lime juice. Taste and adjust the seasoning with more of each if necessary.

Cook the rice noodles according to the package instructions, then plunge into cold water and separate to stop them from sticking. When ready to serve, bring the broth to a rolling boil, distribute the noodles into bowls topped with the sliced raw beef fillet. While the broth is bubbling, ladle it into the bowls so it poaches the beef and warms the noodles.

Serve immediately and scatter the beansprouts, spring onions/scallions, herbs, limes and chillies/chiles over the top.

NOTE: You can make this without the bones using beef stock instead. Simply add 2 litres/4 pints of beef stock to a pot with the ginger, onion and all the spices. Bring to the boil and then simmer for about 45 minutes–1 hour to reduce. Then follow the rest of the instructions above.

250 g/9 oz. dried rice stick
    noodles
2 large skinless chicken
    breast fillets
1 litre/2 pints chicken stock
2 tablespoons vegetable oil
400 ml/1²/₃ cups coconut milk
200 ml/³/₄ cup coconut cream
2 tablespoons fish sauce
2 teaspoons caster/
    granulated sugar

LAKSA PASTE
6 shallots, chopped
4 garlic cloves, chopped
2 lemongrass stalks, thinly
    sliced
2 large red bird's eye chillies/
    chiles, deseeded and sliced
a 2.5-cm/1-inch piece of fresh
    galangal, chopped
a 2.5-cm/1-inch piece of fresh
    turmeric, chopped, or 1
    teaspoon ground turmeric
4 macadamia nuts
1 tablespoon shrimp paste
2 teaspoons coriander seeds,
    toasted and ground

TO SERVE (OPTIONAL)
beansprouts, trimmed
¹/₂ cucumber, sliced
Deep-fried Shallots (page 12)
fresh coriander/cilantro
1 lime, cut into wedges
Sambal Olek (page 10) or
    Chilli/Chili Oil (page 11)

SERVES 4

CHICKEN LAKSA

Laksa is a spicy noodle soup made with coconut milk and either pork, chicken or seafood. It is always adorned with a selection of garnishes. Malaysian food draws on its rich heritage of cultures from Chinese to Indian and these combine here with the use of spices, herbs and coconut to create a truly unique soup.

Soak the noodles in a bowlful of hot water for 20–30 minutes until softened. Drain well, shake dry and set aside.

Put the chicken breast in a saucepan with the stock and set over a low–medium heat. Simmer very gently for 10 minutes until the chicken is just cooked. Remove the chicken from the stock and set aside to cool completely. Once cool, slice thinly.

To make the laksa paste, pound all the ingredients together in a large pestle and mortar or blitz in a food processor until smooth.

Heat the oil in a wok or non-stick saucepan set over a medium heat and add the laksa paste. Fry for 2 minutes until fragrant, then add the coconut milk and chicken stock. Simmer gently for 10 minutes, then stir in the coconut cream, fish sauce and sugar. Simmer gently for a further 2–3 minutes.

Divide the noodles between bowls and add the sliced chicken. Pour over the hot soup and serve topped with a selection of garnishes. Pass around a pot of sambal olek or a bottle of chilli/chile oil, to drizzle.

VEGETABLE AND CHICKEN RAMEN

2 skinless, boneless chicken
  breasts, sliced into thin
  strips
100 g/3^1/$_2$ oz. soba noodles
2 tablespoons brown rice
  miso paste
1 tablespoon soy sauce
a 2-cm/^{3}/$_4$-inch piece of fresh
  ginger, cut into thin strips
1 carrot, julienned
3 spring onions/scallions,
  sliced diagonally
^{1}/$_2$ red (bell) pepper, deseeded
  and cut into thin strips
2 pak choi/bok choy, halved
  lengthways
^{1}/$_2$ teaspoon toasted sesame oil
a pinch of toasted nori flakes
2 tablespoons fresh
  coriander/cilantro leaves
sunflower oil, for brushing

SERVES 2

Don't be put off by the long list of ingredients for this ramen – the Japanese-style soup couldn't be easier to make and is light, soothing and nourishing. It includes iodine-rich nori (a type of seaweed) and miso as its base (this healthy soya-bean paste is most often sold in health-food shops).

Preheat the grill/broiler to high and line the grill pan with foil.

Arrange the chicken in the grill pan and brush with sunflower oil. Grill/broil for 5–6 minutes on each side, turning until cooked through and there is no trace of pink in the centre.

Meanwhile, cook the soba noodles in plenty of boiling water following the instructions on the packet, then drain and refresh under cold running water. Set aside.

Put 750 ml/1^1/$_2$ pints of hot water into a saucepan, add the miso paste and stir until dissolved. Add the soy sauce, ginger, carrot, spring onions/scallions, red (bell) pepper and pak choi/bok choy and bring up to boiling point. Reduce the heat and simmer for about 3 minutes until the pak choi/bok choy is just tender. Stir in the sesame oil.

Divide the noodles between 2 shallow bowls and spoon over the vegetables and stock. Slice the chicken breasts and place on top, sprinkle with the nori and coriander/cilantro leaves, then serve.

BEEF PHO

1 kg/2 lb. beef short ribs
a 5-cm/2-inch piece of fresh
   ginger, sliced and pounded
1 onion, sliced
2 garlic cloves, sliced
3 whole star anise, pounded
2 cinnamon sticks, pounded
400 g/14 oz. dried rice stick
   noodles
350 g/12 oz. thinly sliced beef
   fillet
3 tablespoons fish sauce
1 teaspoon salt
1 teaspoon caster/granulated
   sugar
freshly squeezed juice
   of 1 lime
125 g/2$^1/_3$ cups beansprouts,
   trimmed

GARNISHES

2 red bird's eye chillies/
   chiles, chopped
a handful each of fresh Thai
   basil, Vietnamese mint and
   coriander/cilantro
6 spring onions/scallions,
   trimmed and sliced

SERVES 4

It is the large baskets of colourful herbs and condiments that give this classic soup its freshness and that unique flavour and texture. To allow the flavours to develop, you need to prepare this dish a day in advance.

Put the short ribs in a large saucepan, cover with cold water and bring to the boil. Simmer for 10 minutes then drain and wash the ribs. Return them to the pan and add 2 litres/4 pints more cold water along with the ginger, onion, garlic, star anise and cinnamon. Return to the boil and simmer gently for 1$^1/_2$ hours, or until the meat is tender.

Carefully remove the ribs from the stock and set aside to cool. Thinly shred the meat, discarding the bones. Strain the stock through a fine-mesh sieve/strainer and set aside to cool. Refrigerate both the meat and the stock overnight.

The next day, soak the noodles in a bowlful of hot water for 20–30 minutes, until softened. Drain well, shake dry and divide the noodles between large bowls.

Meanwhile, skim and discard the layer of fat from the cold stock and return the pan to a medium heat until just boiling. Stir in the shredded meat, beef fillet, fish sauce, salt, sugar and lime juice. Place the beef fillet on the noodles, spoon over the stock and top with the beansprouts.

Serve with a plate of the garnishes alongside for everyone to help themselves.

2 tablespoons salt
1 kg/2¼ lbs. rib of beef
500 g/1 lb. beef shin/flank
600 g/1 lb. 5 oz. chopped,
    boneless oxtail
2 litres/4 pints chicken stock
1 large onion, peeled and both
    ends trimmed
6 lemongrass stalks, bashed
40 g/1½ oz. rock sugar
1 daikon/mooli, peeled
1 tablespoon salt
1 tablespoon shrimp paste
1 tablespoon pork bouillon
1 bún bò huế stock cube
    (optional)
4 tablespoons fish sauce
3 tablespoons cooking oil
½ bulb of garlic cloves, finely
    chopped
2 lemongrass stalks, finely
    diced
½ teaspoon chilli/chili
    powder
½ tablespoon annatto powder
450 g/1 lb. thick rice
    vermicelli noodles
2 spring onion/scallions,
    thinly sliced
½ red onion, thinly sliced
8 sprigs of coriander/
    cilantro, roughly chopped
chã chiên Vietnamese ham,
    thinly sliced
lime wedges, to serve

SERVES 6–8

HUẾ NOODLE SOUP WITH BEEF AND PORK

Bún bò huế, originates from Huế (the city of temples, emperor's palaces and dynasties in central Vietnam) and is spicy, bold and invigorating.

Bring a pot of water to the boil with the salt. Add the meat and bones, and boil for about 10 minutes until scum forms on the surface. Remove from the heat and discard the water. Wash the meat in cold water, removing any scum, and set aside. This will give a clearer broth.

Wash the pan, add 3 litres/5½ pints of fresh water and bring to the boil. Return the meat and bring to a gentle simmer. Skim off any scum and fat from the surface with a spoon. Add the chicken stock.

Now heat a stove-top griddle pan over a high heat (do not add oil). Char the onion and lemongrass stalks on both sides. Add these to the broth with the sugar, daikon/mooli and salt. Simmer for at least 2 hours with the lid on. Check it occasionally and skim off any scum and fat from the surface.

After 2 hours, remove the beef from the pan and allow it to rest slightly, then slice thinly and store in an airtight container until serving. Add the shrimp paste, pork bouillon, stock cube (if using) and fish sauce to the broth.

In another pan, heat the oil and fry the garlic, diced lemongrass and chilli/chili powder. Add this to the broth with the annatto powder and simmer.

Put the noodles in a saucepan with a lid, cover with boiling water and apply lid. Leave for 20 minutes or according to package instructions. Drain and rinse with hot water.

Mix the spring onions/scallions, red onion and coriander/cilantro together. Put a serving of vermicelli in a big, deep soup bowl. Put the cooked beef and Vietnamese ham on top and sprinkle with the onion mixture. Bring the broth to boiling point and pour over the noodles to submerge them.

Squeeze lime into the soup and serve with a variety of garnishes.

SHIO RAMEN WITH PORK AND EGGS

1 tablespoon sake
1 tablespoon mirin
1 garlic clove, crushed
1 teaspoon grated fresh
   ginger
50 ml/¼ cup dark soy
   sauce
50 ml/¼ cup light soy
   sauce
1 tablespoon caster/
   granulated sugar
750 g/1½ lb. pork belly,
   skin removed
4 eggs
2 litres/4 pints chicken
   or pork stock
250 g/9 oz. dried ramen
   noodles
spring onions/scallions,
   thinly sliced to
   garnish

SERVES 4

Also known as 'tonkotsu', this ramen is rich in flavour from homemade chicken or pork broth with additional savoury notes of soy, sweetened with sugar. The pork belly is braised in an Asian marinade that marries perfectly with the slightly soft boiled/cooked egg. Spring onions/scallions add a dose of freshness to this hearty noodle soup.

Pour the sake and mirin into a small saucepan set over a medium heat and bring slowly to the boil. Add the garlic, ginger, dark and light soy sauces and the sugar, and stir until the sugar dissolves. Bring to the boil and simmer very gently for 5 minutes. Remove from the heat and leave to cool.

Cut the pork belly in half across the grain to make two similar squares and put in a saucepan into which the pork fits snugly.

Pour over the cooled soy mixture, return to the heat and bring to the boil. Cover and simmer gently for 1 hour or until the pork is tender. Remove the pan from the heat but leave the pork in the stock to cool at room temperature. Remove the pork from the stock, reserving the stock, and cut into thick slices. Set aside.

Put the eggs in a saucepan of cold water and set over a high heat. Bring to the boil and simmer for 5 minutes. Remove the eggs from the pan and immediately rinse under cold running water until they are cool enough to handle. Peel the eggs and place them in a clean bowl. Pour over the reserved pork stock and leave to soak for 30 minutes. Lift the eggs from the stock and cut in half lengthways.

Meanwhile bring the chicken stock to the boil in a large saucepan and simmer until reduced by about one-third. Remove from the heat and stir in 4 tablespoons of the reserved pork stock. Add the pork belly slices and warm for 5 minutes.

Plunge the noodles into a saucepan of boiling water, return to the boil and cook for about 4 minutes or until al dente. Drain well, then divide the noodles between soup bowls. Spoon over the stock and pork slices, add 2 egg halves to each bowl and serve garnished with spring onions/scallions.

CHICKEN NOODLE SOUP

200 g/7 oz. dried Hokkein
  noodles
1.25 litres/2¹/₂ pints chicken
  stock
2 teaspoons grated fresh
  ginger
2 tablespoons light soy sauce
2 tablespoons shaoxing rice
  wine
1 tablespoon oyster sauce
200 g/7 oz. chicken breast
  fillet, sliced
about 6 pak choi/bok choy,
  trimmed and roughly
  chopped
2 spring onions/scallions,
  trimmed and thinly sliced,
  plus extra to serve
salt, to taste

GARNISHES (OPTIONAL)
fresh chillies/chiles, sliced
a small bunch of fresh
  coriander/cilantro

SERVES 4–6

It's no wonder chicken soup is known for its soothing medicinal properties as well as its flavour — it tastes so good and so healthy with an underlying hint of ginger and garlic from the stock. This is a simple soup, but with a really good stock as a base it's hard to beat.

Plunge the noodles into a saucepan of boiling water and cook for 3–4 minutes until al dente. Drain, refresh under cold water and shake dry. Set aside.

Pour the stock into a large saucepan with the ginger, soy sauce, rice wine and oyster sauce and set over a medium heat. Bring slowly to the boil, then simmer for 5 minutes.

Stir in the chicken, pak choi/bok choy and spring onions/scallions, and simmer for 3–4 minutes until the chicken is cooked.

Divide the noodles between bowls, pour over the chicken soup and serve with some sliced chillies/chiles and fresh coriander/cilantro, if using.

TIP: If using fresh Hokkein noodles cook for 2 minutes instead of 3–4. If using vacuum-packed, pre-cooked noodles rinse under boiling water only before use. For either you will need 500 g/1 lb.

FISH AND SEAFOOD

HOT AND SOUR FISH SOUP

200 g/9 oz. cellophane
    noodles
6 kaffir lime leaves, torn
1 large red chilli/chile,
    roughly chopped
a 2.5-cm/1-inch piece of fresh
    ginger, chopped
1 lemongrass stalk, trimmed
    and roughly chopped
2 garlic cloves
1.5 litres/3 pints chicken
    stock
2 shallots, finely chopped
500 g/1 lb. fish steaks or
    fillets, such as striped bass
    or bream
50 g/1 cup spinach, torn
4 tablespoons Jeow Marg
    Leng (page 10), plus extra
    to serve
freshly squeezed juice of 1
    lime
2 tablespoons fish sauce
a bunch of fresh coriander/
    cilantro

SERVES 4

Unlike those of its neighbours, Lao cuisine tends to be sour and salty rather than sweet, sour and salty like this one. The addition of the roasted tomato salsa adds a fiery heat to the soup and a light smokey flavour. This would traditionally be made with river fish such as catfish or carp but you can use whatever fish you like.

Soak the noodles in a bowlful of hot water for 10 minutes until softened. Drain well, shake dry and set aside.

Put the lime leaves, chilli/chile, ginger, lemongrass and garlic in a pestle and mortar and pound together until fragrant – it should still be quite bitty. Transfer this paste to a saucepan set over a medium heat and pour over the stock. Bring to the boil then simmer gently for 20 minutes until really fragrant.

Add the shallots and simmer for 5 minutes, then carefully add the fish fillets and cook gently for 4–5 minutes until cooked through. Remove the pan from the heat and stir in the spinach, jeow marg leng, lime juice, fish sauce and coriander/cilantro. Cover with a lid and set aside for 5 minutes to allow the flavours to develop.

Divide the noodles between bowls and carefully spoon the fish on top, pour over the soup and serve at once with extra jeow marg leng.

350 g/11½ oz. dried rice
    vermicelli noodles
2 litres/4 pints chicken stock
4 tablespoons fish sauce
2 tablespoons grated palm
    sugar
250 g/9 oz. skinless white
    fish fillets, such as cod,
    ling or pollock
250 g/9 oz. cleaned squid
    bodies
250 g/about 25 medium
    prawns/shrimp
250 g/about 15 scallops
250 g/about 25 fresh clams
    (or about 10 mussels),
    cleaned
125 g/1½ cups choi sum

TO SERVE
a handful each of fresh Thai
    basil, mint and coriander/
    cilantro
red chillies/chiles, sliced
2 limes, cut into wedges

SERVES 6

SEAFOOD STEAMBOAT

Most Asian countries make some sort of large seafood hotpot and Malaysia is no different. It is a wonderfully warming, exotic dish that should be shared.

Soak the noodles in a bowlful of hot water for 10–20 minutes until softened. Drain well, shake dry and set aside.

Pour the stock into a large saucepan set over a medium heat. Add the fish sauce and sugar and bring to the boil. Once boiling, reduce the heat but keep warm.

Next prepare the seafood. Remove any bones from the fish and cut into 2.5-cm/1-inch cubes. Open out the squid body by cutting down one side and score the inside flesh with a sharp knife in a diamond pattern. Cut into 2.5-cm/1-inch pieces.

Peel the prawns/shrimp, leaving the tail section intact. Cut down the back of each one almost in half and pull out the black intestinal tract. Wash and dry the prawns/shrimp and set aside.

Trim the grey muscle from the side of each scallop and set aside.

Arrange all the seafood, cooked noodles and choi sum on a large platter on the table.

Place a portable gas burner in the middle of the table and pour half the chicken stock into a smaller saucepan. Bring to a gentle simmer (keeping the remaining stock warm on the stove). Place the bowls of garnishes next to each guest along with a serving bowl and noodles.

Using tongs, the guests can then cook the seafood and choi sum in the hot stock, which will become increasingly flavoursome. As the food cooks, spoon it into the serving bowls with some noodles and a little of the stock and top with fresh herbs, chillies/chiles and lime juice. Top up with more stock as required.

8 large prawns/shrimp

1.5 litres/3 pints Dashi Broth (page 8)

125 ml/¹/₂ cup Japanese soy sauce

75 ml/scant ¹/₃ cup mirin

250 g/9 oz. dried ramen noodles

2 handfuls mangetout/snow peas, trimmed and thinly sliced

2 tablespoons dried wakame seaweed

150 g/5¹/₂ oz. firm tofu, cubed

2 large spring onions/ scallions, trimmed and thinly sliced

vegetable oil, for deep-frying

TEMPURA BATTER

1 egg yolk

250 ml/1 cup iced water

100 g/³/₄ cup plain/ all-purpose flour

2 tablespoons potato or rice flour

SERVES 4

RAMEN WITH TEMPURA SHRIMP

Like all Japanese dishes it is the contrast of textures and flavours that defines this dish. The soft slurp of noodles is balanced with the crisp tempura batter which, once submerged into the hot stock, becomes soft, gooey and comforting to eat.

Peel the prawns/shrimp, leaving the tail section intact and reserving the shells and head. Cut down the back of each one and pull out the black intestinal tract. Wash and dry the prawns/shrimp and set aside. Put the shells and heads in a saucepan set over a medium heat and pour in the broth. Bring to the boil, cover and simmer for 30 minutes. Strain through a fine mesh sieve/strainer and return the stock to the pan. Add the soy sauce and mirin and set aside.

Plunge the noodles into a saucepan of boiling water and cook for about 4 minutes, or until al dente. Drain, refresh under cold water and shake dry. Set aside.

To make the tempura batter, put the egg yolk, iced water and both flours in a large mixing bowl. Very lightly beat the mixture together using a fork to make a slightly lumpy but thin batter.

Return the broth mixture to a simmer, add the mangetout/snow peas and seaweed and simmer for 2 minutes. Add the noodles and cook for 1 minute to heat through.

Meanwhile heat about 5 cm/2 inches of oil in a wok or old saucepan until a cube of bread dropped into the oil crisps and turns brown in 20–30 seconds. Dip the prawns/shrimp into the tempura batter, shaking off any excess. Fry in batches for 2–3 minutes until crisp and golden. Carefully remove the cooked prawns/shrimp and drain on paper towels. Add a little of the remaining tempura batter to the oil and cook until crisp. Drain this and put with the prawns/shrimp.

Divide the noodles between warmed soup bowls, add the tofu and spring onions/ scallions, then pour over the soup. Top each with two tempura prawns/shrimp and sprinkle the crispy batter bits into the soup. Serve at once.

400 g/14 oz. dried rice
 vermicelli noodles
4 tablespoons Asian dried
 shrimp
2 tablespoons peanut oil
4 shallots, thinly sliced
2 garlic cloves, crushed
2 red chillies/chiles,
 deseeded and finely
 chopped
4 tomatoes, deseeded and
 coarsely chopped
200 g/7 oz. cooked white
 crabmeat, flaked
1.25 litres/2$\frac{1}{2}$ pints chicken
 stock
2 tablespoons Asian fish
 sauce
1 teaspoon soft brown sugar
1 tablespoon rice vinegar
$\frac{1}{2}$ iceberg lettuce, thinly
 sliced

TO SERVE
2 spring onions/scallions,
 finely chopped
a handful of fresh coriander/
 cilantro leaves
a handful of mint leaves
1 lime, cut into wedges

SERVES 4

VIETNAMESE CRAB NOODLE SOUP

This aromatic noodle soup is a speciality of central Vietnam, where all productive land is given over to cultivating rice. The authentic recipe uses tiny freshwater crabs commonly found in paddy fields that are pounded to a paste and made into dumplings, but here, for ease, the crabmeat floats freely in the soup. You don't even have to go crab hunting, use fresh or frozen prepared white crabmeat.

Put the noodles into a bowl and cover with boiling water for 10 minutes, or until soft. Drain, rinse under cold running water and drain again. Using kitchen scissors, chop them into manageable lengths, about 5 cm/2 inches, and set aside.

Put the dried shrimp into another bowl, add 125 ml/$\frac{1}{2}$ cup boiling water and soak for 20 minutes. Drain and reserve the shrimp and their soaking water.

Heat the oil in a wok, swirl to coat, then add the shallots, garlic and chillies. Stir-fry for 1 minute, then add the tomatoes, crabmeat, soaked shrimp, their soaking water and the chicken stock. Season the soup with fish sauce, sugar and vinegar and bring to the boil. Reduce the heat to low and let simmer for 5 minutes.

Turn off the heat and stir in the noodles and lettuce.

Ladle the soup into 4 bowls and serve with the spring onions/scallions, coriander/cilantro and mint leaves and lime wedges on top.

4 Asian shallots, halved

4 garlic cloves (skin on)

4 large red chillies/chiles

1 kg/2 lb. smoked gammon
knuckle

a 5-cm/2-inch piece of fresh
galangal, sliced

6 kaffir lime leaves, pounded

2 tablespoons fish sauce

250 g/9 oz. dried rice
vermicelli noodles

$\frac{1}{2}$ small green papaya,
peeled and shredded

50 g/$\frac{1}{3}$ cup drained and
sliced bamboo shoots
(optional)

$\frac{1}{4}$ Chinese cabbage, thinly
sliced

5–6 snake beans, trimmed
and thinly sliced

250 g/9 oz. river fish fillets,
such as trout or perch

TO SERVE

2 limes, cut into wedges

fresh chillies/chiles, chopped

fresh Thai basil leaves

SERVES 4–6

VERMICELLI SOUP WITH RIVER FISH

Being landlocked, Laos makes best use of its many rivers and the fish that
thrive there. This is typical of the type of fish soup that is eaten daily in Laos.
Traditionally, the stock would be flavoured with a ham hock, the meat being
added to the soup, but gammon knuckle gives a wonderfully smokey flavour.

Preheat a stovetop ridged grill pan over a medium heat until it's smoking hot. Arrange
the shallots cut-side down in the pan along with the garlic cloves and chillies/chiles.
Char-grill for 5 minutes, turn over and cook for a further 5 minutes until everything
is well charred.

Place the gammon in a large saucepan with 3 litres/5$\frac{1}{2}$ pints of cold water, the charred
vegetables, the galangal, kaffir lime leaves and fish sauce. Set over a high heat and
bring to the boil. Simmer gently for 1$\frac{1}{2}$ hours, skimming any scum from the surface.
Carefully remove the gammon, discard the skin and cut the meat into shreds. Set aside.

Soak the noodles in a bowlful of hot water for 20 minutes until softened. Drain well and
arrange on a platter with the papaya, bamboo shoots, cabbage and snake beans.

Return the shredded meat to the stock and add the fish, simmer gently
for 2–3 minutes until the fish is cooked. Stir in the noodles and sliced snake beans.

Serve the soup from the pan so everyone can
help themselves to the noodles, vegetables,
herbs and other garnishes.

250 g/9 oz. dried rice stick
 noodles
350 g/11 oz. bream or
 snapper fillets, cut into
 2.5-cm/1-inch pieces
250 ml/1 cup chicken stock
125 ml/¹/₂ cup coconut cream
125 ml/¹/₂ cup coconut milk
1 tablespoon fish sauce
2 teaspoons grated palm
 sugar

LEMONGRASS PASTE

6 lemongrass stalks
a 2.5-cm/1-inch piece of fresh
 galangal, peeled and
 roughly chopped
a 2.5-cm/1-inch piece of
 turmeric, peeled and
 roughly chopped
2 kaffir lime leaves, shredded
2 garlic cloves, roughly
 chopped
2 tablespoons chopped
 peanuts
1 teaspoon shrimp paste
1 teaspoon freshly grated
 ginger

TO SERVE

¹/₂ cucumber, sliced
60 g/1 cup beansprouts
lotus root (optional)

SERVES 4

NUM BÁNH CHOK

'Khmer noodles' is the generic name given to num bánh chok, a classic Cambodian soup traditionally served at breakfast or as an afternoon snack. Although you will find regional differences it is always made with a freshly pounded lemongrass paste, fish, noodles and a selection of crisp raw vegetables and fresh herbs.

Soak the noodles in a bowlful of hot water for 20 minutes until softened. Drain well using a kitchen cloth and set aside.

To make the lemongrass paste, discard the hard end of the lemongrass stalk and peel away and discard the hard outer leaves until you reach the soft core of the stalk. Trim lengths of about 5 cm/2 inches and roughly chop the remaining core. Place the lemongrass in a food processor with the remaining ingredients and blend to a smooth paste.

Heat the oil in a wok or saucepan set over a medium heat until it starts to shimmer. Add the paste and fry for 2–3 minutes until fragrant. Add the fish pieces and fry gently for 2 minutes until cooked. Remove the fish from the pan as carefully as you can and set aside.

Add the stock, coconut cream and coconut milk to the pan and simmer gently for 10 minutes until thick and creamy. Stir in the fish sauce and sugar, and simmer for a final minute.

Divide the noodles between bowls and top with the pieces of fish. Pour over the broth and serve with bowls of sliced cucumber, beansprouts and lotus root.

Fishcakes with Dill (page 13),
uncooked
3 tablespoons cooking oil
2 litres/4 pints chicken, pork
or vegetable stock
1/2 teaspoon coarsely ground
black pepper
2 teaspoons sugar
2 teaspoons sea salt
1 teaspoon pork bouillon or
1 chicken stock cube
(optional)
2 tablespoons fish sauce
2 tablespoons cooking oil
8 Asian shallots, chopped
800 g/1³/₄ lbs. fresh udon
noodles

GARNISHES
Deep-fried Shallots (page 12,
optional)
garden mint, chopped
coriander/cilantro, coarsely
chopped
garlic chives, cut into
2-cm/1-inch pieces
(optional)
dill, finely chopped (optional)
cockscomb mint, torn
(optional)
sliced Bird's Eye chillies/
chiles
lime wedges

SERVES 4

UDON SOUP WITH FISHCAKES

In Phan Thiết in Vietnam, street vendors sell this soup at night. The chicken-stock broth is flavoured by the fishcakes and fried shallots. Dill, mint and lime bring it together to make it the most enticing yet cleansing thing to eat by moonlight. The broth can be made from any stock, and you can use fish fillets, seafood such as prawns/shrimp, crab and squid, and meat such as chicken and pork.

Take two-thirds of the uncooked fishcake mixture (page 13) and shape into a patty. Put 1 tablespoon of the oil in a frying pan/skillet over a medium heat and fry the patty on both sides until golden. Cut it into thin slices.

Pinch off bite-size pieces from the remaining uncooked fishcake mixture and roll into rough balls. Set aside.

Put the stock, pepper, sugar, salt, pork bouillon and fish sauce in a saucepan over a medium heat and bring to a gentle boil.

Meanwhile, put the remaining 2 tablespoons of oil in a frying pan/skillet over a medium heat and fry the shallots until brown and crispy.

Bring another pan of water to the boil and blanch the noodles for 2 minutes. Drain and divide them between 4 soup bowls. Add the slices of fried fishcake and a generous pinch of the chopped herbs from the garnishes. Add more pepper, to taste.

When ready to serve, make sure the pan of broth is still boiling, then add the uncooked fish balls. After a couple of minutes when they have floated to the surface, tip in your fried shallots. Ladle the soup into the prepared soup bowls.

Scatter the remaining herbs, the deep-fried shallots and chillies/chiles over the soup and serve with the lime.

- 200 g/7 oz. dried rice vermicelli noodles
- 1 lemongrass stalk, trimmed and finely chopped
- 2 garlic cloves, roughly chopped
- 2 teaspoons grated fresh ginger
- 1 teaspoon shrimp paste
- 1 tablespoon fish sauce
- 3 tablespoons vegetable oil
- 1 onion, thinly sliced
- 50 g/2 oz. banana stem or canned palm heart, sliced (optional)
- 1 teaspoon ground turmeric
- $1/4$ teaspoon dried red chilli/ hot red pepper flakes
- 250 g/9 oz. skinless white fish fillet, finely chopped or minced
- 1.25 litres/$2^1/2$ pints chicken stock
- 40 g/$1/2$ cup chickpea/gram flour, toasted

GARNISHES

- 2 hard-boiled/hard-cooked eggs, peeled and finely chopped
- 2 tablespoons Deep-fried Shallots (page 12)
- 2 tablespoons Sambal Olek (page 10)

SERVES 4

MOHINGA

Burmese food is full of influences from its neighbouring countries and their cultures, but also present are Indian influences like ground spices and chickpea/ gram flour used as a thickening agent. Mohinga is an aromatic noodle soup served mainly for breakfast. In fact, Mohinga is considered by many as Myanmar's national dish and is served at hawkers' stalls all over the country.

Soak the noodles in a bowlful of hot water for 10–20 minutes until softened.

Drain well, shake dry and set aside.

Grind the lemongrass, garlic, ginger, shrimp paste and fish sauce together in a pestle and mortar or food processor to form a thin paste.

Heat the oil in a saucepan set over a medium heat and gently fry the onion and banana stem, if using (leave the palm hearts until later), for 5 minutes until softened. Stir in the turmeric and chilli/hot red pepper flakes and cook for 1 minute. Add the lemongrass paste and fry for a further 5 minutes.

Add the fish and cook, stirring continuously, until golden. Pour in the stock and bring to the boil.

Meanwhile, combine the toasted chickpea/gram flour with 2 tablespoons cold water in a bowl until smooth. Stir in 3–4 tablespoons of the hot stock and then whisk the whole lot back into the soup. Bring to the boil, stirring continuously, and simmer for 5 minutes.

Divide the noodles between serving bowls. Spoon over the soup and serve with a large platter of the garnishes.

SALMON AND MISO SOUP

a small bunch of spring
    onions/scallions
2 salmon fillets
100 g/3¹/₂ oz. dried noodles
a handful of edamame beans
2 tablespoons miso paste or
    powder
400 ml/³/₄ pint hot water

SERVES 2

This simple, stress-free soup is perfect after a long day and can be knocked up in a just a few minutes. The quickest recipe for ramen that you are likely to find!

Boil a kettle full of water. Finely chop the spring onions/scallions.

Put a non-stick frying pan/skillet over a medium heat. Once hot, put the salmon fillets in, skin-side down – you don't need any oil. Let them cook without prodding or poking, you'll see the dark pink flesh of the salmon get lighter. Once the flesh near the middle has cooked, using a fish slice, turn the fillet over. Let it cook for a little bit longer (2–3 minutes) ideally keeping the inside of the fillet a little bit darker than the outside.

Use the boiling water in the kettle to fill a saucepan and cook the noodles according to the packet instructions. Throw the edamame beans in at the end to cook for a couple of minutes.

Stir miso powder or paste into the hot water.

The amount of miso you use is up to you, have a taste and see how strong you want it – check the information on the packet for guidance.

Put the chopped spring onions/scallions into the miso to warm them through.

Strain the noodles and edamame beans, and divide them between 2 bowls. Place the salmon on top of the noodles and pour the miso broth over the top.

INDEX

Assam laksa 24

beef: beef pho 39
  hue noodle soup with beef
    and pork 40
  Vietnamese pho 32
broths: basic broths 8–9
  kombu broth with tempura
    28

cabbage: quick kimchi 11
chicken: chicken broth 9
  chicken laksa 35
  chicken noodle soup 44
  Sapporo miso ramen with
    chicken 31
  vegetable and chicken
    ramen 36
chilli/chili oil 11
crab: Vietnamese crab
  noodle soup 52

dashi broth 8

eggs: boiled/cooked 11
  shio ramen with pork and
    eggs 43

fish: fishcakes with dill 13
  hot and sour fish soup 47
  mohinga 60
  num banh chok 56
  salmon and miso soup 63
  seafood steamboat 48
  udon soup with
    fishcakes 59
      vermicelli soup
        with river fish 55
      fish sauce,
        vegan 11

hot and sour fish soup 47
hue noodle soup with beef
  and pork 40

jeow marg leng 10

kimchi, quick 11
kombu broth with tempura
  28

laksa: Assam laksa 24
  chicken laksa 35

miso paste: miso ramen 16
  salmon and miso soup 63
  Sapporo miso ramen with
    chicken 31
mohinga 60
mung bean vegetable
  noodle soup 27
mushroom udon 19

num banh chok 56
nuts, crushed roasted 12

oil, chilli/chili 11

pho: beef pho 39
  Vietnamese pho 32
pork: hué noodle soup with
  beef and pork 40
  shio ramen with pork and
    eggs 43
prawns/shrimp: ramen with
  tempura shrimp 51

sambal olek 10
Sapporo miso ramen with
  chicken 31
sauces 10–11
seafood steamboat 48
shallots, deep-fried 12
shio ramen with pork and
  eggs 43
shrimp, ramen with tempura
  51
somen noodles with wasabi
  and dipping sauce, chilled
    20
soups: chicken noodle soup
  44

fragrant vegetable Siam
  soup 23
hot and sour fish soup 47
hue noodle soup with beef
  and pork 40
mung bean vegetable
  noodle soup 27
noodle soup with crispy
  tofu 15
salmon and miso soup 63
udon soup with fishcakes
  59
vermicelli soup with river
  fish 55
Vietnamese crab noodle
  soup 52
steamboat, seafood 48

tempura: kombu broth with
  tempura 28
  ramen with tempura
    shrimp 51
tofu: noodle soup with
  crispy tofu 15
  two ways with tofu 13

udon noodles: mushroom
  udon 19
udon noodle soup with
  crispy tofu 15
udon soup with fishcakes
  59

vegan fish sauce 11
vegetables: fragrant
  vegetable Siam soup 23
  miso ramen with stir-fried
    vegetables 16
  mung bean vegetable
    noodle soup 27
  vegetable and chicken
    ramen 36
  vegetable broth 8
Vietnamese crab noodle
  soup 52
Vietnamese pho 32

wasabi, chilled somen
  noodles with 20

RECIPE CREDITS

Miranda Ballard
Bone Broth

Kimiko Barber
Chilled Somen Noodles with Wasabi and
  Dipping Sauce
Sapporo Miso Ramen with Chicken
Vietnamese Crab Noodle Soup

Jordan Bourke
Udon Noodle Soup with Crispy Tofu
Traditional Vietnamese Pho

Ross Dobson
Miso Ramen with Stir-fried Vegetables

Nicola Graimes
Soba with Chicken and Vegetables

Dunja Gulin
Kombu Broth with Tempura

Jackie Kearney
Assam Laksa
Deep-fried Puffed Tofu
Fragrant Vegetable Siam Soup
Marinated Tofu
Mung Bean Noodle Soup
Vegan Fish Sauce

Uyen Luu
Fishcakes with Dill
Hue Noodle Soup with Beef and Pork
Udon Noodle Soup with Fishcakes

Claire and Lucy Macdonald
Salmon and Miso Soup

Louise Pickford
Beef Pho
Chicken Broth
Chicken Laksa
Chilli/Chili Oil
Dashi Broth
Deep-fried Shallots
Hot and Sour Fish Soup
Jeow Marg Leng
Mohinga
Mushroom Udon
Num Banh Chok
Ramen with Tempura Shrimp
Sambal Olek
Seafood Steamboat
Shio Ramen with Pork and Eggs
Vermicelli Soup with River Fish

Belinda Williams
Vegetable Broth